EGYPT
VISUAL SOURCEBOOK

FOR ARTISTS, ARCHITECTS, AND DESIGNERS

EGYPT
VISUAL SOURCEBOOK

Jim Hewitt

FOR ARTISTS, ARCHITECTS, AND DESIGNERS

The American University in Cairo Press
Cairo ◆ New York

First published in 2011 by
The American University in Cairo Press
113 Sharia Kasr el Aini, Cairo, Egypt
420 Fifth Avenue, New York, NY 10018
www.aucpress.com

Dar el Kutub No. 11253/10
ISBN 978 977 416 433 0

Dar el Kutub Cataloging-in-Publication Data

Hewitt, Jim
    Egypt Visual Sourcebook / Jim Hewitt. —Cairo: The American University in Cairo Press, 2011
    p.   cm.
    For Designers, Architects, and Artists.
    ISBN 978 977 416 433 0
    1. Architecture—Egypt I. Title
    720.962

1 2 3 4 5 6   14 13 12 11

Concept by Jim Hewitt
Design by Andrea El-Akshar
Layout and CD design by Cherif Abdullah
Printed in Egypt

CONTENTS

Introduction   3

1: Photo Plates
Cairo Citadel   8
Coptic Cairo   22
Cairo Bazaar   46
Streets and Buildings   60
Giza Pyramids   112
Saqqara Pyramid   122
Abu Simbel Temple   130
Kom Ombo Temple   142
Edfu Temple   156
Luxor Temple   170
Karnak Temple   180
Philae Temple   190
Mount Sinai   206
Saint Catherine's Monastery   216

2: Typologies
Arches   232
Mihrabs   238
Doorways   239
Windows   246
Wall Embellishments   258
Corbels   262
Wooden Brackets   264
Lighting   268
Balconies and Screens   271
Railings   274
Rooflines   278
Domes   282
Minarets   284
Columns   288
Column Capitals   294

3: Details and Surfaces

Balconies and Screens 306
Column Capitals 310
Statues 314
Bas-relief 321
Hieroglyphs/Carved 329
Hieroglyphs/Painted 336
Architecture 338
Tile 346
Fabric 347
Wood 348
Metal 350
Screens and Grillwork 352
Wall Surfaces/Composite 354
Wall Surfaces/Stone 357
Wall Surfaces/Brick and Block 360
Wall Surfaces/Stucco 366
Stone Surfaces 368
Natural Stone Surfaces 371

4: Graphics

Street Graphics 374
Packaging 382

Bibliography 384
Chronology 386

INTRODUCTION

During a recent trip to Egypt, I was fascinated by the design elements I saw throughout the country, and I noticed how aspects of the ancient and modern combined to create some of the most culturally-rich architecture I had ever seen. Egyptian architecture has clearly influenced design in my country, as well others throughout the world. It makes sense, really, as Egypt is home to one of the oldest cultures in history, and since its wonders were first revealed, the magnificent imprint of Egyptian artistic innovations has been widely recognized.

As a set designer/art director for movies and television, I realized how useful it would be to have a book documenting these design elements that I and my colleagues could use in the course of our work. As the book developed, it turned into more than just a simple reference book, but became a visual guide to Egyptian architecture for everyone.

The *Egypt Visual Sourcebook* was designed to present the complexities of Egyptian architecture in a user-friendly format. It is for people who have traveled to Egypt, students who are working on school projects, interested readers who love the myriad aspects of the Egyptian aesthetic, and for professional art directors.

Within the Plates section, you will find comprehensive photographs from sites around Egypt. The color versions are also presented in black-and-white form and labeled with a number/letter combination. This tag refers to the page and position where you will find these elements enlarged within the Typologies, Details and Surfaces, and Graphics sections.

In the Typologies section, photographs are grouped by category (for example, Balconies, Archways, Rooftops).

The Details and Surfaces section features close-ups from the Plates in categories such as Column Capital, Wall Surfaces, and Tiles.

The final section of the book is Graphics, with photographs of signs, banners, and packaging from all over the country.

The accompanying CD contains image files of all the color photographs in the book. These files can be used for ease of reference in design work, and as a basis for redrafting for incorporation into design or art projects. (They may not be used directly for commercial purposes or published in any form without the prior written permission of the publisher.)

As I examined my collection of photographs, I realized some of them seemed to inaccurately show the size of their subjects, so I have added a 1.8 m (6 ft) scale human silhouette or a 20 cm (8 in) scale hand silhouette to some images in order to help clarify the sizing.

I hope these images will transport you to Egypt. Every time I look at them, I'm reminded how architecture and culture are intertwined, and our lives are not complete without appreciating both.

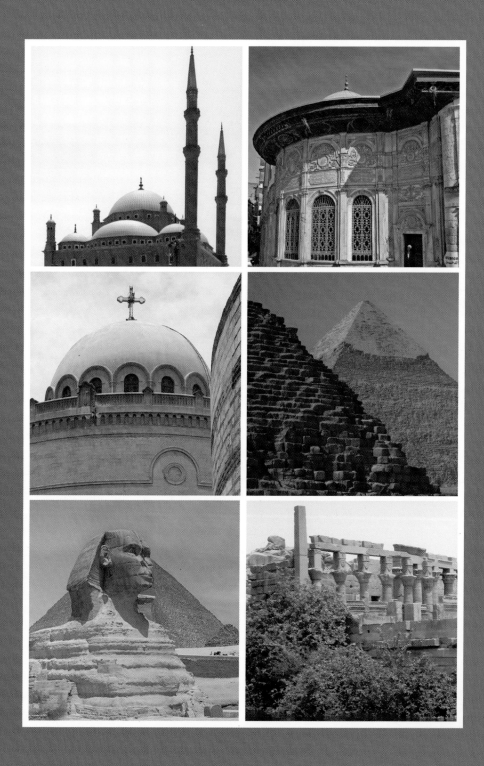

1

PHOTO PLATES

CAIRO CITADEL

View of Cairo from the Citadel, toward the dome of the Madrasa of Sultan Hasan, (left)
and the al-Rifa'i Mosque, 19th century (right).

9

285A

283H

287E

247C

247D

235D

236A

302B

Muhammad 'Ali Mosque, the Citadel, Cairo. Ottoman style, 1832–1857.

Muhammad 'Ali Mosque interior, the Citadel, Cairo. Ottoman style, 1832–1857.

Muhammad 'Ali Mosque interior, the Citadel, Cairo. Ottoman style, 1832–1857.

Muhammad 'Ali Mosque dome detail, the Citadel, Cairo. Ottoman style, 1832–1857.

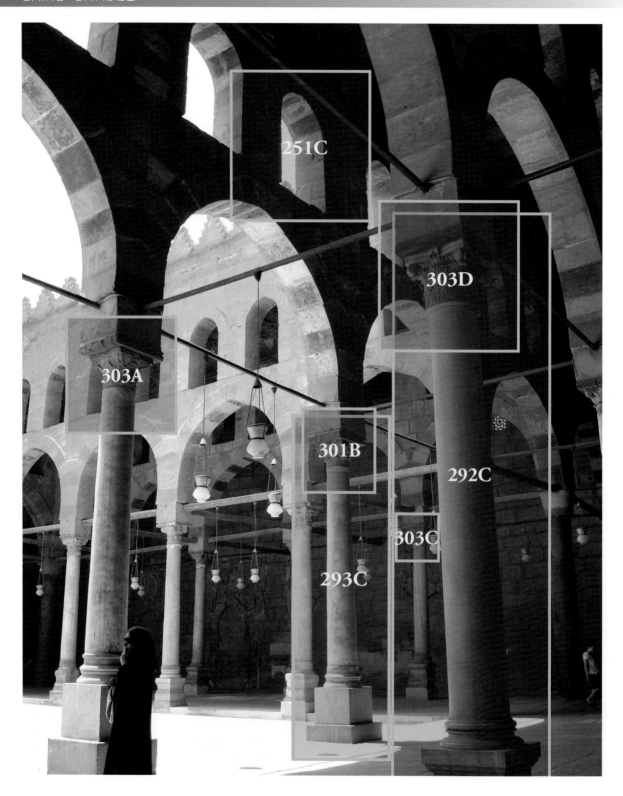

Sultan al-Nasir Muhammad Mosque courtyard, the Citadel, Cairo. Mamluk, 1318–1335 (showing original Ptolemaic, Christian, and Roman columns).

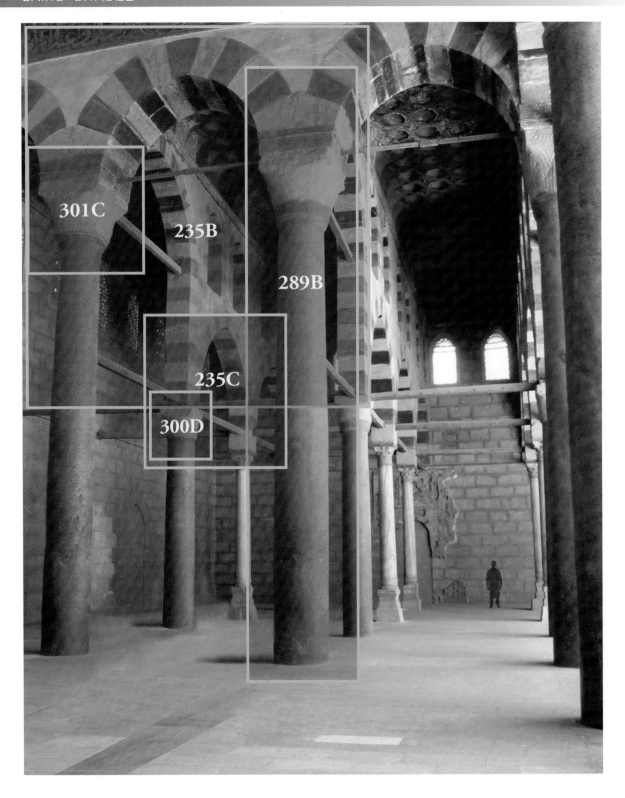

301C

235B

289B

235C

300D

Sultan al-Nasir Muhammad Mosque interior, the Citadel, Cairo. Mamluk, 1318–1335 (showing original Ptolemaic, Christian, and Roman columns).

COPTIC CAIRO

The Hanging Church (al-Mu'allaqa) façade, Old Cairo. Coptic Christian, 19th century.

The Hanging Church (al-Mu'allaqa) interior, Old Cairo. Coptic Christian, 11th century, with 19th-century restoration.

The Hanging Church (al-Mu'allaqa) interior, Old Cairo. Coptic Christian,
11th century, with 19th-century restoration.

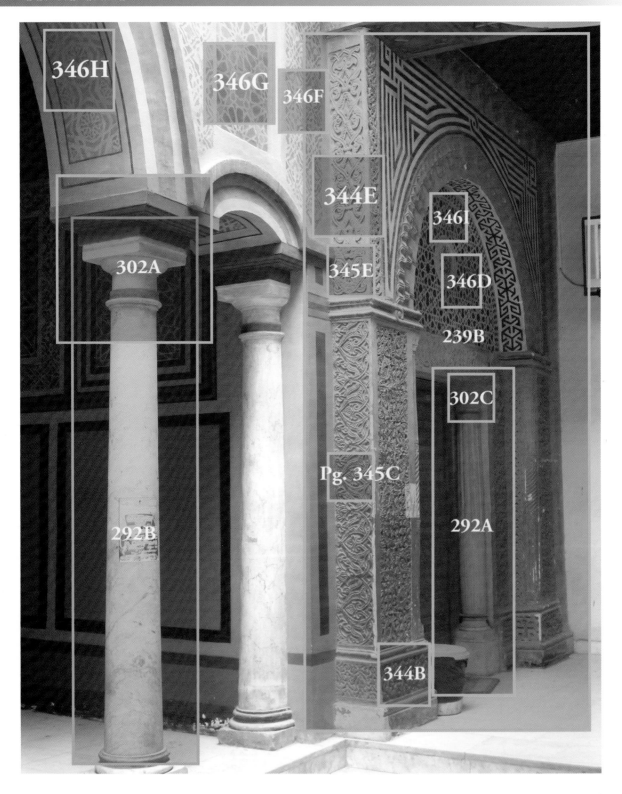

The Hanging Church (al-Mu'allaqa) interior, Old Cairo. Coptic Christian, 11th century, with 19th-century restoration.

Passageway in Old Cairo. Ancient and modern walls.

Passageway in Old Cairo. Ancient and modern walls.

Passageway and arch in Old Cairo. Ancient and modern walls.

Stairway in Old Cairo.

Door leading to the Greek Orthodox Church of St. George, Old Cairo. Early 20th century.

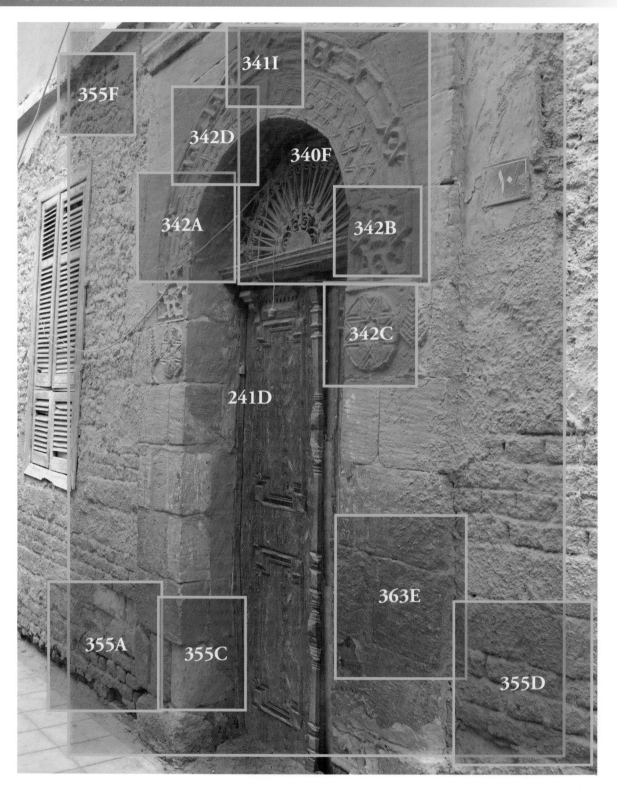

Doorway on street in Old Cairo.

Doorway on street in Old Cairo.

Doorway on street in Old Cairo.

Doorway to the Church of Saints Sergius and Bacchus (Abu Serga), Old Cairo.
Late 7th century AD.

CAIRO BAZAAR

Badistan Gate in Khan al-Khalili Bazaar. Upper part: late Mamluk, 1511;
lower part: Ottoman period.

Gate of al-Ghuri in the Khan al-Khalili Bazaar.
The arch beyond it is the Gate of the Wikala of al-Ghuri. Late Mamluk, 1511.

Spice shop in the Khan al-Khalili Bazaar.

Street scene, Khan al-Khalili Bazaar.

Street scene, Khan al-Khalili Bazaar.

Street scene, Khan al-Khalili Bazaar.

South of the Khan al-Khalili Bazaar, looking south toward the twin minarets of the al-Mu'ayyad Sheikh complex next to Bab Zuwayla.

Perfume shop, Khan al-Khalili Bazaar.

STREETS AND BUILDINGS

Donkey carts, Cairo.

View looking south toward the twin minarets of the al-Mu'ayyad Sheikh complex (Mamluk, 1415–20) on the gate of Bab Zuwayla, Cairo.

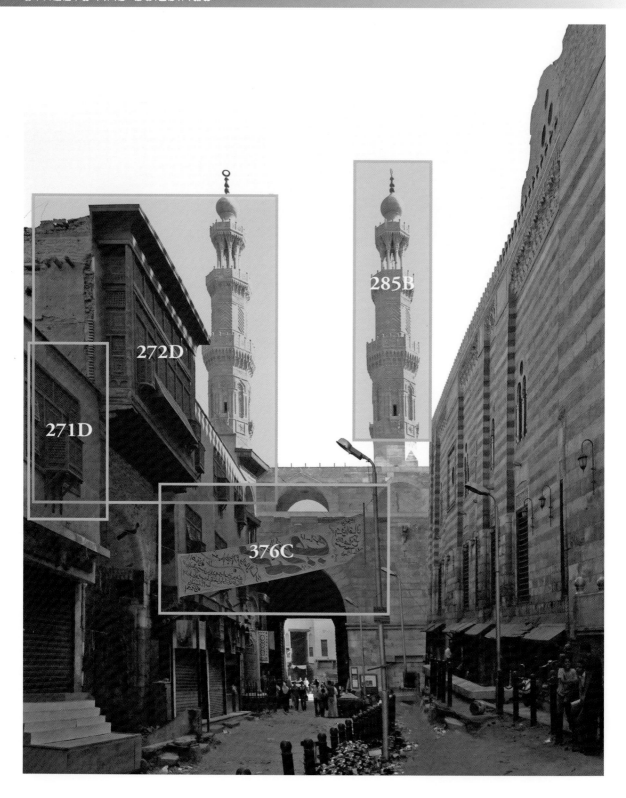

al-Muʻizz li-Din Allah Street, looking south toward Bab Zuwayla, Fatimid, 1092.
On right, the al-Muʻayyad Sheikh complex, Cairo. Mamluk, 1415–20.

282C

263A

66

Near the Street of the Tentmakers (al-Khayamiya), Cairo.
On left: Mosque of Mahmud al-Kurdi.

Traditional scaffolding between two buildings,
Street of the Tentmakers (al-Khayamiya), Cairo.

At the beginning of the restored Street of the Tentmakers (al-Khayamiya),
Cairo. Ottoman, 1650.

The restored Street of the Tentmakers (al-Khayamiya), Cairo. Ottoman, 1650.

Residential street, Luxor.

Residential street, Cairo.

Wall on residential street, Cairo.

Market, Bahariya Oasis, Western Desert.

Local market, Luxor.

Local market, Luxor.

Local market, Luxor.

Local market, Luxor.

Local market, Luxor.

Local street, Luxor.

Nineteenth-century residential building next to modern building, Cairo.

257D

257B

273B

273D

367A

257A

Early 20th-century residential building near the Citadel, Cairo.

Turned-wood mashrabiya window on a restored Ottoman residential building near
Khan al-Khalili, Cairo.

Nineteenth-century residential/commercial building, Cairo.

361I

361F

249A

367F

365G

267D

367H

Modern residential/commercial building, Cairo.

The Greek Orthodox Church of St. George, Old Cairo (early 20th century).
Built on top of the Babylon Fortress, Roman, 3rd century AD.

Sabil-Kuttab of Tusun Pasha (also known as the Sabil-Kuttab of Muhammad 'Ali), Cairo. 1820.

The Sabil (water dispensary) of Nafisa al-Bayda, Cairo. 1796.

278B
279B
235A
248B
287G
284C
287H
261D
261B
283A
279C
279A
259D

Minarets of al-Azhar Mosque, Cairo. Mamluk, 15–16th century. At left: 20th century neo-Islamic building, 1939.

Abu al-Haggag Mosque, Luxor. 19th-century restoration.

Abu al-Haggag Mosque, Luxor. Original 13th century with 19th-century restoration.

GIZA PYRAMIDS

Left to right: Khafre's Valley Temple, the Pyramid of Khafre, and the Sphinx, Giza.
4th Dynasty, 2575–2450 BC.

Pyramid of Menkaure, Giza. 4th Dynasty, 2575–2450 BC.

Entrance to the Pyramid of Khufu, Giza. 4th Dynasty, 2575–2450 BC.

Top: Pyramids of Kuhfu (left) and Khafre (right). Bottom: Pyramids of Khafre (left) and Menkaure (right), Giza. 4th Dynasty, 2575–2450 BC.

117

The Sphinx, Giza. 4th Dynasty, 2575–2450 BC.

SAQQARA PYRAMID

Step Pyramid of Djoser, Saqqara. 3rd Dynasty, 2650–2575 BC.

362G

362I

127

Step Pyramid of Djoser, Saqqara. Foreground: complex of restored ceremonial buildings
to the south of the pyramid. 3rd Dynasty, 2650–2575 BC.

Step Pyramid of Djoser, Saqqara. 3rd Dynasty, 2650–2575 BC.

ABU SIMBEL TEMPLE

Ramesses Temple, Abu Simbel. 19th Dynasty, 1244–1224 BC.

Hathor Temple of Queen Nefertari, Abu Simbel. 19th Dynasty, 1244–1224 BC.

Ramesses Temple, Abu Simbel. 19th Dynasty, 1244–1224 BC.

Hathor Temple of Queen Nefertari, Abu Simbel. 19th Dynasty, 1244–1224 BC.

328A

316B

136

316D

243B

Entrance to the Ramesses Temple, Abu Simbel. 19th Dynasty, 1244–1224 BC.

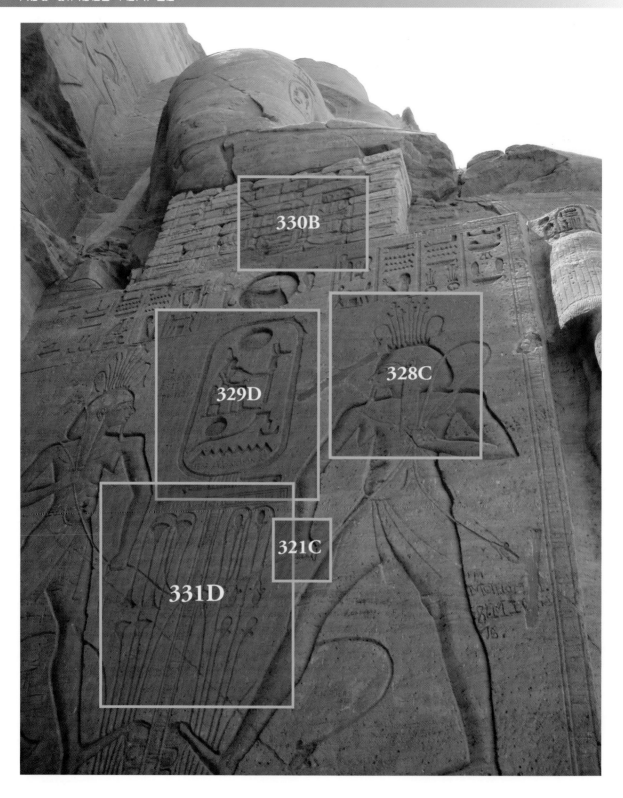

330B

329D

328C

321C

331D

Hieroglyphs to the right of the entrance to the Ramesses Temple,
Abu Simbel. 19th Dynasty, 1244–1224 BC.

315B

View from the doorway of the Ramesses Temple, Abu Simbel.
19th Dynasty, 1244–1224 BC.

KOM OMBO TEMPLE

View of the outer hypostyle hall from the forecourt area, Temple of Haroeris and Sobek, Kom Ombo. Ptolemy VI, 180–145 BC.

Column in outer hypostyle hall, Temple of Haroeris and Sobek,
Kom Ombo. Ptolemy VI, 180–145 BC.

Doorway to the inner hypostyle hall, Temple of Haroeris and Sobek,
Kom Ombo. Ptolemy VI, 180–145 BC.

145

Ceiling in outer hypostyle hall, Temple of Haroeris and Sobek,
Kom Ombo. Ptolemy VI, 180–145 BC.

334A

334D

334B

334C

323D

323B

323C

323A

scale

Bas-relief of Sekhmet in outer corridor, Temple of Haroeris and Sobek,
Kom Ombo. Ptolemy VI, 180–145 BC.

Outer corridor, Temple of Haroeris and Sobek, Kom Ombo. Ptolemy VI, 180–145 BC.

Wall foundation, Temple of Haroeris and Sobek, Kom Ombo. Ptolemy VI, 180–145 BC.

Wall tie (butterfly clamp) connection, Temple of Haroeris and Sobek, Kom Ombo.
Ptolemy VI, 180–145 BC.

EDFU TEMPLE

Entry pylon, Temple of Horus, Edfu. Ptolemy IX, 88–81 BC.

Hypostyle hall entrance (above), entry pylon (below), Temple of Horus, Edfu.
Ptolemy VII and IX, 145 BC and 116 BC.

Columns in the Hypostyle Festival Hall, Temple of Horus, Edfu.
Ptolemy VII and IX, 145 BC and 116 BC.

The Hypostyle Festival Hall and entrance to the Sanctuary (right), Temple of Horus, Edfu. Ptolemy VII and IX, 145 BC and 116 BC.

Hall of Offerings and Sanctuary, Temple of Horus, Edfu.
Ptolemy VII and IX, 145 BC and 116 BC.

Reliefs and hieroglyphs in the external corridor, Temple of Horus, Edfu.
Ptolemy VII and IX, 145 BC and 116 BC.

Reliefs and hieroglyphs in the external corridor, Temple of Horus, Edfu.
Ptolemy VII and IX, 145 BC and 116 BC.

Reliefs and hieroglyphs in the Hall of Offerings, Temple of Horus, Edfu.
Ptolemy VII and IX, 145 BC and 116 BC.

Typical wall corner and cornice, Temple of Horus, Edfu.
Ptolemy VII and IX, 145 BC and 116 BC.

LUXOR TEMPLE

Entry pylon, Luxor Temple, Luxor. 19th Dynasty, 1279–1213 BC.

314D

Court of Ramesses II, Luxor Temple, Luxor. 18th/19th Dynasty, 1319–1279 BC.

320B
320D
327A
320C
327C
320A

Statues of Ramesses II, Luxor Temple, Luxor. 19th Dynasty, 1279–1213 BC.

289A

327B

Columns in the Court of Ramesses II, Luxor Temple, Luxor. 19th Dynasty, 1279–1213 BC.

KARNAK TEMPLE

Entry pylon, Precinct of Amun, Karnak, Luxor. 25th Dynasty, 650 BC.

316C

361B

321A

Ram statues in the Forecourt, Precinct of Amun, Karnak, Luxor. 25th Dynasty, 650 BC.

Hypostyle Hall, Precinct of Amun, Karnak, Luxor. 19th Dynasty, 1290–1213 BC.

Columns in the Hypostyle Hall, Precinct of Amun, Karnak, Luxor.
19th Dynasty, 1290–1213 BC.

Columns in the Hypostyle Hall, Precinct of Amun, Karnak, Luxor.
19th Dynasty, 1290–1213 BC.

Columns in the Central Court and Sanctuary, Precinct of Amun, Karnak, Luxor.
19th Dynasty, 1290–1213 BC.

PHILAE TEMPLE

Temple of Isis, Philae. Egyptian Greco-Roman, 300 BC – AD 200.

Western colonnade, Temple of Isis, Philae. Egyptian Greco-Roman, 300 BC – AD 200.

312A

294C

313A

294C

289C

Western colonnade, Temple of Isis, Philae. Egyptian Greco-Roman,
300 BC – AD 200.

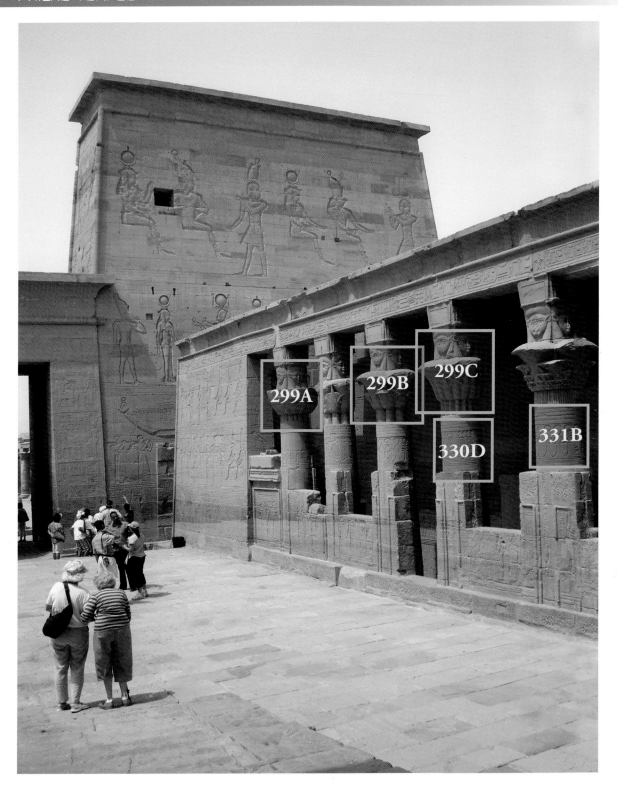

View from the Forecourt toward the first pylon and the Birth House,
Temple of Isis, Philae. Egyptian Greco-Roman, 300 BC – AD 200.

Hieroglyphs on the first pylon, Temple of Isis, Philae. Egyptian Greco-Roman, 300 BC – AD 200.

East entrance into the Forecourt, Temple of Isis, Philae. Egyptian Greco-Roman, 300 BC – AD 200.

Temple of Isis, Birth House with first and second pylons, Philae. Egyptian Greco-Roman, 300 BC – AD 200.

Temple of Isis, west and east colonnades with first pylon, Philae. Egyptian Greco-Roman, 300 BC – AD 200.

200
245B

Temple of Isis, eastern entrance into Forecourt, Philae. Egyptian Greco-Roman,
300 BC – AD 200.

MOUNT SINAI

Chapel of the Holy Trinity, Mount Sinai, Sinai Peninsula. Greek Orthodox, 1934
(originally built AD 500).

Chapel of the Lady of the Storehouse, Mount Sinai, Sinai Peninsula.
Byzantine, 6th century.

Elijah's Gate and the Steps of Repentance, Mount Sinai, Sinai Peninsula.
Byzantine, 6th century.

Kiosks selling souvenirs at the top of Mount Sinai, Sinai Peninsula.

Elijah's Basin, Mount Sinai, Sinai Peninsula. Byzantine, 6th century.

St. Catherine's Monastery, Mount Sinai, Sinai Peninsula. Greek Orthodox, AD 537.

SAINT CATHERINE'S MONASTERY

Saint Catherine's Monastery, Mount Sinai, Sinai Peninsula.
Greek Orthodox, AD 537.

358E

256D 359E

360G

362A

Exterior wall of Saint Catherine's Monastery, Mount Sinai, Sinai Peninsula.
Greek Orthodox, AD 537.

Marketplace at the entrance to Saint Catherine's Monastery, Mount Sinai,
Sinai Peninsula. Greek Orthodox, AD 537.

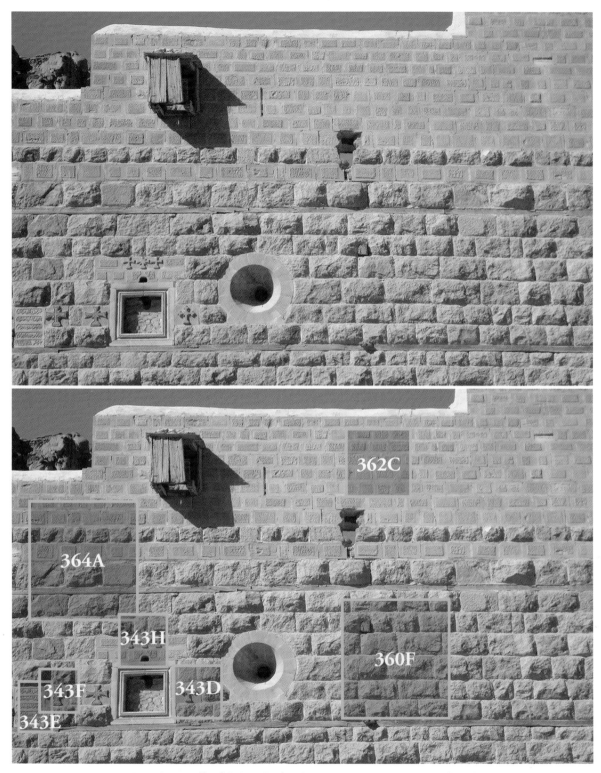

Exterior wall of Saint Catherine's Monastery, Mount Sinai,
Sinai Peninsula. Greek Orthodox, AD 537.

221

Entrance to Saint Catherine's Monastery, Mount Sinai, Sinai Peninsula.
Greek Orthodox, AD 537.

Inner courtyard and door, Saint Catherine's Monastery, Mount Sinai,
Sinai Peninsula. Greek Orthodox, AD 537.

223

The Burning Bush, Saint Catherine's Monastery, Mount Sinai, Sinai Peninsula.
Greek Orthodox, AD 537.

Interior wall of Saint Catherine's Monastery, Mount Sinai, Sinai Peninsula.
Greek Orthodox, AD 537.

Interior wall, Saint Catherine's Monastery, Mount Sinai, Sinai Peninsula.
Greek Orthodox, AD 537.

2
TYPOLOGIES

A. Gate of the Wikala of al-Ghuri in the Khan al-Khalili Bazaar, Cairo. Late Mamluk, 1511. See 48 and 340D.

B. Gate of al-Ghuri in the Khan al-Khalili Bazaar. The arch beyond it is the Gate of the Wikala of al-Ghuri. Late Mamluk, 1511. See page 48 and 341E.

C. Badistan Gate, Khan al-Khalili Bazaar, Cairo. Ottoman. See page 46 and 341F.

D. Bab Zuwayla, Cairo. Fatimid,1092.

A. Sultan al-Nasir Muhammad Mosque, the Citadel, Cairo. Mamluk, 1318–1335.

B. Trilobed arch, upper part of Badistan Gate, Khan al-Khalili Bazaar, Cairo. Late Mamluk, 1511.

C. al-Mu'izz li-Din Allah Street, Cairo. Ottoman, late 18th century.
See page 102 for context.

D. Modern arch, al-Mu'izz li-Din Allah Street, Cairo.

A. Pointed arch, Old Cataract Hotel, Aswan. Neo-Islamic, 1899.

B. Keel arch, Old Cataract Hotel, Aswan. Neo-Islamic, 1899.

C. Horseshoe arch, Old Cataract Hotel, Aswan. Neo-Islamic, 1899.
See page 341H.

D. Old Cataract Hotel, Aswan. Neo-Islamic, 1899.

A. al-Azhar Mosque, Cairo. Neo-Islamic, 1939. See page 104.

B. Sultan al-Nasir Muhammad Mosque, the Citadel, Cairo. Mamluk, 1318–1335. See page 18.

C. Sultan al-Nasir Muhammad Mosque, the Citadel, Cairo. Mamluk, 1318–1335. See page 18.

D. Muhammad 'Ali Mosque, the Citadel, Cairo. Ottoman style, 1832–1857. See page 10.

A. Muhammad 'Ali Mosque, the Citadel, Cairo. Ottoman style, 1830–1848. See page 10.

B. Muhammad 'Ali Mosque, the Citadel, Cairo. Ottoman style, 1830–1848.

C. The Hanging Church (al-Mu'allaqa), Old Cairo. Coptic Christian, 11th Century, with 19th-century restoration.

D. The Hanging Church (al-Mu'allaqa), Old Cairo. Coptic Christian, 11th Century, with 19th-century restoration.

A. The Hanging Church (al-Mu'allaqa), Old Cairo. Coptic Christian, 11th Century.

B. The Hanging Church (al-Mu'allaqa), Old Cairo. Coptic Christian, 11th Century. See page 24.

C. The Hanging Church (al-Mu'allaqa), Old Cairo. Coptic Christian, 11th Century. See page 26.

D. The Hanging Church (al-Mu'allaqa), Old Cairo. Coptic Christian, 11th Century. See page 26.

A. Sultan al-Nasir Muhammad Mosque, the Citadel, Cairo. Mamluk, 1318–1335. See page 346E.

B. Sayyidna al-Hussein Mosque, Cairo. Neo-Islamic, 19th century.

C. al-Azhar Mosque, Cairo. Mamluk, 1363.

A. Sayyidna al-Hussein Mosque, Cairo. Neo-Islamic, 19th century. See 340I, 341B, 344G, 351 A–I.

B. The Hanging Church (al-Mu'allaqa), Old Cairo. Coptic Christian, 11th Century. See page 28, 302C, 339H, 342E, 344B, 345A–C, E, H, 346D, I, 348C, F.

C. The Hanging Church (al-Mu'allaqa), Old Cairo. Coptic Christian, 11th Century. See page 291C, 339G,I, 344B, 345 A, C, G, I, 349G.

D. Sayyidna al-Hussein Mosque, Cairo. Neo-Islamic, 19th century. See page 350A–I, 365E.

A. Sabil-Kuttab of Tusun Pasha (also known as the Sabil-Kuttab of Muhammad 'Ali), Cairo. 1820. See page 100 and 340C.

B. al-Azhar Mosque, mid-18th century. See page 340B, 344D, H.

C. The Egyptian Museum, Cairo. 1904. See page 340H, 365F.

D. The Egyptian Museum, Cairo. 1904. See page 365F.

A. Doorway leading to the Greek Orthodox Church of St. George, Old Cairo. Early 20th century. See page 34, 267B, 349D,F, 365D.

B. Doorway in Old Cairo near the Greek Orthodox Church of St. George. See page 38, 340E, 342G, 344F, I.

C. Doorway in Old Cairo. See page 348D.

D. Doorway in Old Cairo. See page 36, 340F, 341I, 342A–D, 355A, C, D, 363E.

A. Street of the Tentmakers (al-Khayamiya), Cairo.

B. Street of the Tentmakers (al-Khayamiya), Cairo.

C. St. Catherine's Monastery, Mount Sinai, Sinai Peninsula. Greek Orthodox, AD 537. See page 357I, 270D.

D. Luxor Temple, Luxor. 19th Dynasty, 1279–1213 BC.

A. St. Catherine's Monastery, Mount Sinai, Sinai Peninsula. Greek Orthodox, AD 537.

B. The Temple of Ramesses II, Abu Simbel. 19th Dynasty, 1244–1224 BC. See page 134.

C. Elijah's Gate, Mt. Sinai, Sinai Peninsula. See page 210 for context.

D. Valley Temple of Khafre, Giza. 4th Dynasty, 2575–2450 BC. See page 368l, and 112 for context.

A. Luxor Temple, Luxor. 19th Dynasty, 1279–1213 BC.

B. Temple of Isis, Philae. Egyptian Greco-Roman, 300 BC – AD 200.

C. Temple of Horus, Edfu. Ptolemy IX,116 BC.

D. Temple of Horus, Edfu. Ptolemy IX, 116 BC.

A. Entrance to the Pyramid of Khufu, Giza. 4th Dynasty, 2575–2450 BC. See page 116.

B. Temple of Isis, Philae. Egyptian Greco-Roman, 300 BC – AD 200. See page 200, 338D, 339F, 342I, 343G.

C. Luxor Temple, Luxor. 19th Dynasty, 1279–1213 BC.

D. Temple of Haroeris and Sobek, Kom Ombo. Ptolemy VI, 180–145 BC. See page 145.

A. al-Azhar Mosque, Cairo. Neo-Islamic, 1939. See page 291A, 345D, F.

B. St. Catherine's Monastery, Mount Sinai, Sinai Peninsula. Greek Orthodox, AD 537.

C. al-Azhar Mosque, Cairo. Neo-Islamic, 1939. See page 259A, 340A, 343B.

D. Sabil-Kuttab of Tusun Pasha (also known as the Sabil-Kuttab of Muhammad 'Ali), Cairo. 1820. See page 100, 340C, 352H.

A. Muhammad 'Ali Mosque, the Citadel, Cairo. Ottoman, 1830–1848. See page 253A, 352A, C, D, I.

B. The Sabil (water dispensary) of Nafisa al-Bayda, Cairo. 1796. See page 102, 353A, E, F.

C. Muhammad 'Ali Mosque, the Citadel, Cairo. Ottoman, 1830–1848. See page 10, 352B, E, F, G.

D. Muhammad 'Ali Mosque, the Citadel, Cairo. Ottoman, 1830–1848. See page 10, 352A, C, D, I.

A. Local building, Cairo. Twentieth-century Romanesque revival with Islamic turned wood details.

B. al-Azhar Mosque, Cairo. Neo-Islamic, 1939. See page 104, 340G.

C. Greek Orthodox Church of St. George, Old Cairo. Early 20th century. See page 98.

D. Local building, Cairo.

A. Local building, Cairo. See page 96, 365G.

B. Local building, Cairo. See page 74.

C. St. Catherine's Monastery, Mount Sinai, Sinai Peninsula. Greek Orthodox, AD 537. See page 224.

D. Local building, Cairo.

A. Local building, Bahariya Oasis, Western Desert.

B. Old Cairo.

C. Local building, Cairo. See page 353I, 364H.

D. Khan al-Khalili Bazaar, Cairo. See page 48.

A. Old Cairo.

B. Old Cataract Hotel, Aswan. Mamluk revival, 1899.

C. Sultan al-Nasir Muhammad Mosque, the Citadel, Cairo. Mamluk, 1318–1335.

D. Sultan al-Nasir Muhammad Mosque, the Citadel, Cairo. Mamluk, 1318–1335. See page 16 and 18 for context.

A. Abu al-Haggag Mosque, Luxor. Original 13th century, with 19th-century restoration. See page 108.

B. Abu al-Haggag Mosque, Luxor. Original 13th century, with 19th-century restoration. See page 108.

C. Old Cairo, Coptic Christian area. See page 40.

D. Ben Ezra Synagogue, Old Cairo. 1892.

A. Muhammad 'Ali Mosque, the Citadel, Cairo. Ottoman, 1830–1848. See page 10, 247A, 352A, C, D, F, I.

B. Church of Saints Sergius and Bacchus (Abu Serga), Old Cairo. Late 7th century AD, with 19th-century restoration. See page 42, 353D.

C. Building on al-Mu'izz li-Din Allah Street, Cairo. See page 353C, 365C.

D. al-Azhar Mosque, Cairo.

A. Building on al-Mu'izz li-Din Allah Street, Cairo. Mamluk-style detail over window.

B. Badistan Gate in Khan al-Khalili Bazaar. Late Mamluk, 1511. See page 46, 233B.

C. Khan al-Khalili Bazaar, Cairo. Late Mamluk, second half of 15th century.

D. Sayyidna al-Hussein Mosque, Cairo. Neo-Islamic, 19th century. See page 353B, H.

A. Temple of Horus, Edfu. Ptolemy IX, 116 BC.

B. Nineteenth-century residential/commercial building, Cairo. See page 94.

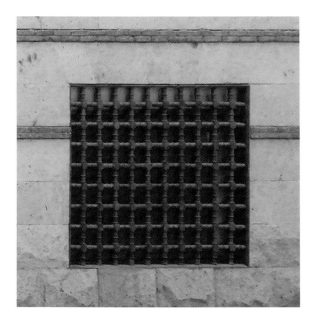

C. Local building, Cairo. See page 353I.

D. Local building, Bahariya Oasis, Western Desert.

A. Local building, Cairo.

B. St. Catherine's Monastery, Mount Sinai, Sinai Peninsula. Greek Orthodox, AD 537. See page 228.

C. St. Catherine's Monastery, Mount Sinai, Sinai Peninsula. Greek Orthodox, AD 537. See page 228.

D. St. Catherine's Monastery, Mount Sinai, Sinai Peninsula. Greek Orthodox, AD 537. See page 218.

A. Early 20th-century residential building near the Citadel, Cairo. See page 90.

B. Early 20th-century residential building near the Citadel, Cairo. See page 90.

C. Nineteenth-century residential building, Cairo. See page 89.

D. Early 20th-century residential building near the Citadel, Cairo. See page 90.

A. Greek Orthodox Church of St. George, Old Cairo. Early 20th century. See page 98.

B. Sayyidna al-Hussein Mosque, Cairo. Fatimid, 11th century.

C. Sabil-Kuttab of Tusun Pasha (also known as the Sabil-Kuttab of Muhammad 'Ali), Cairo. 1820. See page 100.

D. Abu al-Haggag Mosque, Luxor. Original 13th century, with 19th-century restoration. See page 108, 346A–C, 364I.

258

A. al-Azhar Mosque, Cairo. Neo-Islamic, 1939. See page 346C, 339C, 340A, 343B.

B. al-Azhar Mosque, Cairo. Neo-Islamic, 1939. See page 246A, 345D, F (lower section of 259C).

C. al-Azhar Mosque, Cairo. Neo-Islamic, 1939. See page 339B, 345D, F (upper section of 259B).

D. al-Azhar Mosque, Cairo. Nineteenth century. See page 104, 339B, 348I.

A. Sabil-Kuttab of Tusun Pasha (also known as the Sabil-Kuttab of Muhammad 'Ali), Cairo. 1820. See page 100, 340C, 352H.

B. Sabil-Kuttab of Tusun Pasha (also known as the Sabil-Kuttab of Muhammad 'Ali), Cairo. 1820. See page 100, 340C, 240A.

C. Greek Orthodox Church of St. George, Old Cairo. Early 20th century. See page 38.

D. Street in Old Cairo. See page 36.

A. The Sabil (water dispensary) of Nafisa al-Bayda, Cairo. 1796. See page 102 for context, 341C, 344C.

B. Minaret of Sultan al-Ghuri at al-Azhar Mosque, Cairo. Late Mamluk, 1511. See page 104, 284C.

C. Muhammad 'Ali Mosque, the Citadel, Cairo. Ottoman, 1830–1848.

D. Minaret of Emir Aqbugha, al-Azhar Mosque, Cairo. Mamluk, 1340. See page 104, 287H.

A. Restored Ottoman residential building near Khan al-Khalili, Cairo. See page 92.

B. al-Mu'izz li-Din Allah Street, Cairo.

C. al-Mu'izz li-Din Allah Street, Cairo. See page 54.

D. Street of the Tentmakers (al-Khayamiya), Cairo. See page 68.

A. Street of the Tentmakers (al-Khayamiya), Cairo. See page 64, 68.

B. al-Mu'izz li-Din Allah Street, Cairo. See page 102.

C. Old Cairo. See page 40.

D. al-Mu'izz li-Din Allah Street, Cairo.

A. Restored Ottoman residential building near Khan al-Khalili, Cairo. See page 92, 271B.

B. Restored Ottoman residential building near Khan al-Khalili, Cairo. See page 92.

C. Local building, Cairo. See page 271A.

D. Restored Ottoman residential building near Khan al-Khalili, Cairo. See page 92, 272B.

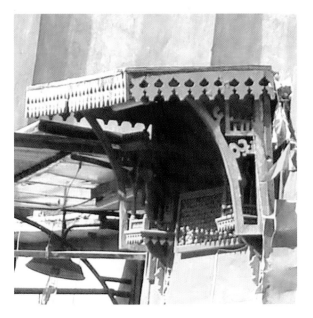

A. Khan al-Khalili, Cairo. See page 51.

B. Khan al-Khalili, Cairo.

C. Khan al-Khalili, Cairo. See page 368H.

D. Khan al-Khalili, Cairo.

A. Old Cairo. See page 40.

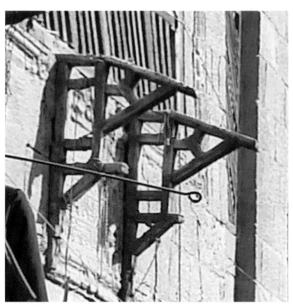

B. Khan al-Khalili Bazaar, Cairo. See page 54.

C. Bahariya Oasis, Western Desert.

D. Khan al-Khalili Bazaar, Cairo.

A. Adjacent to the Hanging Church (al-Mu'allaqa) Old Cairo. Coptic Christian, 19th century. See page 22.

B. Above the doorway leading to the Greek Orthodox Church of St. George, Old Cairo. Early 20th century. See page 34, 241A.

C. St. Catherine's Monastery, Mount Sinai, Sinai Peninsula. Greek Orthodox, AD 330.

D. Modern residential/commercial building, Cairo. See page 96.

A. Hotel lobby, Hurghada.

B. Sofitel Hotel, Sharm al-Sheikh.

C. The Hanging Church (al-Mu'allaqa) interior, Old Cairo. Coptic Christian, 11th century, with 19th-century restoration. See page 24.

D. Sayyidna al-Hussein Mosque, Cairo. Neo-Islamic, 19th century.

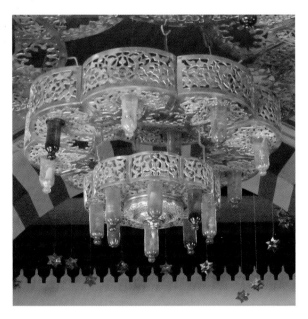

A. Old Cataract Hotel, Aswan.

B. Old Cataract Hotel, Aswan.

C. Old Cataract Hotel, Aswan.

D. Old Cataract Hotel, Aswan.

269

A. St. Catherine's Monastery, Mount Sinai, Sinai Peninsula. Greek Orthodox, AD 537.

B. The Hanging Church (al-Mu'allaqa) interior, Old Cairo. Coptic Christian, 11th century, with 19th-century restoration.

C. St. Catherine's Monastery, Mount Sinai, Sinai Peninsula. Greek Orthodox, AD 537.

D. St. Catherine's Monastery, Mount Sinai, Sinai Peninsula. Greek Orthodox, AD 537. See page 242C.

A. Ottoman-style mashrabiya balcony, Cairo. See page 264C, 308B.

B. Turned-wood mashrabiya window on a restored Ottoman residential building near Khan al-Khalili, Cairo. See page 92, 306D, 264A.

C. al-Mu'izz li-Din Allah Street, Cairo. See page 102, 307B.

D. al-Mu'izz li-Din Allah Street, Cairo. See page 62, 306D, 307A.

271

A. Nineteenth-century residential/commercial building, Cairo. See page 94, 307D.

B. Turned-wood mashrabiya window on a restored Ottoman residential building near Khan al-Khalili, Cairo. See page 92, 306C, 264D.

C. al-Mu'izz li-Din Allah Street, Cairo. See page 102, 308D, 347A, C.

D. al-Mu'izz li-Din Allah Street, Cairo. See page 62, 306A.

A. Old Cataract Hotel, Aswan. See page 307C.

B. Early 20th-century residential building near the Citadel, Cairo. See page 90, 308A.

C. Old Cataract Hotel, Aswan. See page 306B.

D. Early 20th-century residential building near the Citadel, Cairo. See page 90, 308C.

A. Sofitel Hotel, Sharm al-Sheikh.

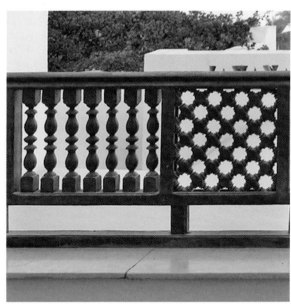

B. Sofitel Hotel, Sharm al-Sheikh.

C. Sofitel Hotel, Sharm al-Sheikh.

D. Sofitel Hotel, Sharm al-Sheikh.

A. The Hanging Church (al-Mu'allaqa) interior, Old Cairo. Nineteenth-century restoration. See page 24.

B. Historic Cairo area.

C. Sofitel Hotel, Sharm al-Sheikh.

D. Local building, Cairo.

A. Local building, Cairo.

B. The Hanging Church (al-Mu'allaqa), Old Cairo. Nineteenth-century restoration. See page 22.

C. Cairo.

D. al-Mu'izz li-Din Allah Street, Cairo. See page 102.

A. Residential street, Cairo. See page 72.

B. Residential street, Cairo. See page 72.

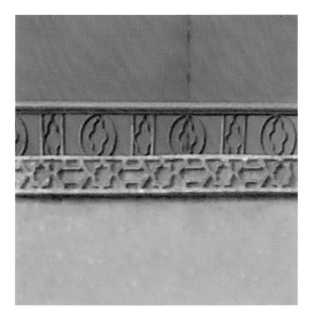

C. Cairo.

D. Near the Hanging Church, Old Cairo.

A. Sabil-Kuttab of Tusun Pasha (also known as the Sabil-Kuttab of Muhammad 'Ali), Cairo. 1820. See page 100.

B. al-Azhar Mosque, Cairo. Neo-Islamic, 1939. See page 104.

C. The Citadel, Cairo.

D. The Citadel, Cairo.

A. al-Azhar Mosque, Cairo. Neo-Islamic, 1939. See page 104.

B. al-Azhar Mosque, Cairo. Neo-Islamic, 1939. See page 104.

C. al-Azhar Mosque, Cairo. Neo-Islamic, 1939. See page 104.

D. Ben Ezra Synagogue, Old Cairo. 1892. See page 339D.

A. Sultan al-Nasir Muhammad Mosque courtyard, the Citadel, Cairo. Mamluk, 1318–1335. See page 16.

B. Abu al-Haggag Mosque, Luxor. Original 13th century with 19th-century restoration. See page 108.

C. St. Catherine's Monastery, Mount Sinai, Sinai Peninsula. Greek Orthodox, AD 537. See page 224.

D. Hotel, Bahariya Oasis, Western Desert.

A. Greek Orthodox Church of St. George, Old Cairo. Early 20th century. See page 98.

B. al-Mu'izz li-Din Allah Street, Cairo. See page 102.

C. Local building, Khan al-Khalili, Cairo.

D. Local building, Cairo. See page 95.

A. Arabesque carving, Ganim al-Bahlawan Mosque. Mamluk, 1510.

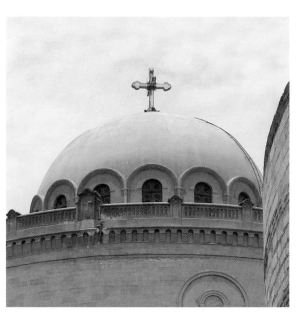

B. Greek Orthodox Church of St. George, Old Cairo. Early 20th century. See page 98.

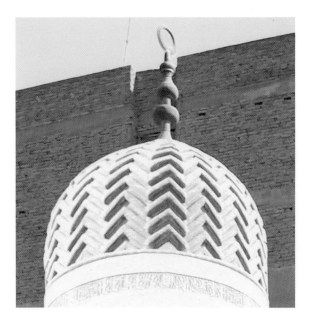

C. Chevron carving, Mahmud al-Kurdi Mosque. Mamluk, 1395. See page 64.

D. St. Catherine's Monastery, Mount Sinai, Sinai Peninsula. Greek Orthodox, AD 537. See page 217.

A. al-Azhar Mosque, Cairo. See page 104.

B. al-Azhar Mosque, Cairo. To the left of Dome A, this page.

C. Sultan Hassan Mosque, Cairo. Restored dome. See page 8.

D. al-Rifa'i Mosque, Cairo. 19th century. See page 9.

E. al-Fath Mosque, Cairo. Late 20th century.

F. Mahmud Pasha Mosque, Cairo. , 1567. See page 8.

G. Amir Akhur Mosque, Cairo. 1503. See page 9, 287F.

H. Muhammad 'Ali Mosque, the Citadel, Cairo. Ottoman style, 1830–1848. See page 10.

A. Sayyidna al-Hussein Mosque, Cairo. Ottoman style, 19th century.

B. al-Mu'ayyad Sheikh minaret. Mamluk, 1419. See page 62, 285B.

C. al-Ghuri minaret, al-Azhar Mosque, Cairo. Mamluk, 1511. See page 104, 261B.

C. Abu al-Haggag Mosque, Luxor. Original 13th century with 19th-century restoration.

A. The Citadel, Cairo. Ottoman style, 1830-1848. See page 11.

B. al-Mu'ayyad Sheikh minaret (on Bab Zuwayla gate). Mamluk, 1419. See page 62, 284B, 363H.

D. Complex of Sultan Qalawun, Bayn al-Qasrayn, Historic Cairo. Early Mamluk, 1284.

A. Sultan al-Nasir
Muhammad Mosque,
the Citadel. Mamluk,
1318.

B. Malika Safiyya
Mosque, Cairo.
Ottoman, 1610.

C. al-Fath Mosque,
Cairo. Late 20th century.

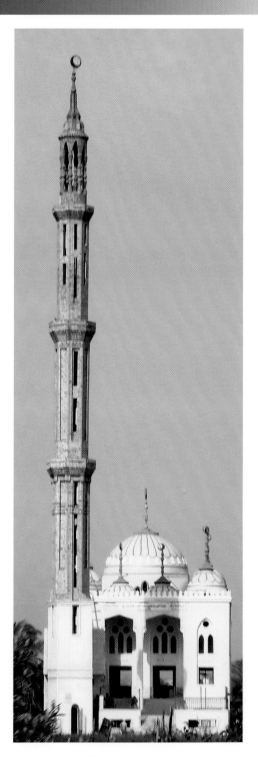

D. Saqqara.

A. Sultan Hassan Mosque. See page 8.

B. Mahmud Pasha Mosque. See page 8.

C. Sultan Hassan Mosque. See page 8.

D. Mahmud Pasha Mosque. See page 8.

E. The Citadel. See page 10.

F. Amir Akhur Mosque. Late Mamluk, 1503. See page 9,283G.

G. al-Azhar Mosque, Qaytbay minaret. Mamluk, 1483. See page 104.

H. al-Azhar Mosque, Aqbugha minaret. Mamluk, 1339.

287

A. Luxor Temple, Luxor. Tentpole. 1279–1213 BC.

B. Precinct of Amun, Karnak, Luxor. Closed papyrus. 1290–1213 BC. See page 187.

C. Precinct of Amun, Karnak, Luxor. Closed papyrus. 1290–1213 BC. See page 186.

A. Luxor Temple, Luxor. 1279–1213 BC. See page 108, 176.

B. Sultan al-Nasir Muhammad Mosque, the Citadel, Cairo. Ptolemaic column. See page 18.

C. Temple of Isis, Philae. Papyrus and lotus. 300 BC – AD 200. See page 194.

A. Temple of Horus, Edfu. Open papyrus. 145 BC. See page 159.

B. Temple of Isis, Philae. Hathor capital. 300 BC – AD 200. See page 192.

C. Precinct of Amun, Karnak, Luxor. Open papyrus. 1400 BC. See page 185.

A. al-Azhar Mosque, Cairo.
See page 246A.

B. al-Azhar Mosque, Cairo.

C. The Hanging Church (al-Mu'allaqa), Old Cairo. See page 239C.

D. al-Azhar Mosque, Cairo.

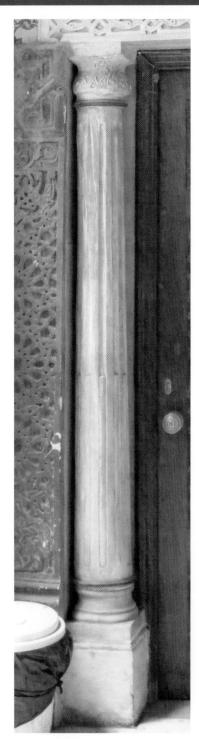

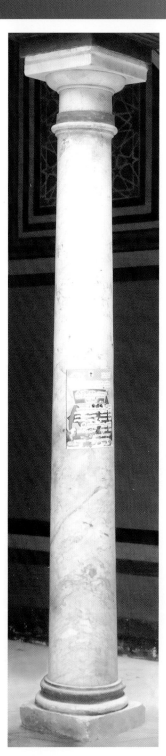

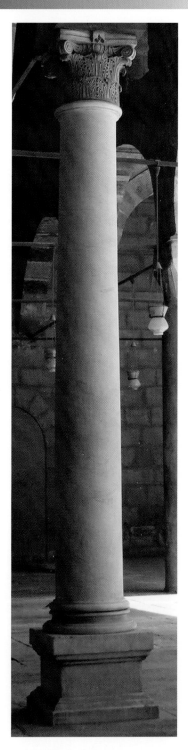

A. The Hanging Church (al-Mu'allaqa), Old Cairo. See page 28.

B. The Hanging Church (al-Mu'allaqa), Old Cairo. Roman Doric. See page 28.

C. Sultan al-Nasir Muhammad Mosque, the Citadel. Roman composite. See page 16.

A. Muhammad 'Ali Mosque, the Citadel, Cairo.

B. The Hanging Church (al-Mu'allaqa), Old Cairo. Roman composite. See page 26.

C. Sultan al-Nasir Muhammad Mosque, the Citadel. Roman composite. See page 16.

293

A. Temple of Isis, Philae. Open lotus. 300 BC – AD 200. See page 310A, 313C.

B. Temple of Isis, Philae. Open lotus. 300 BC – AD 200. See page 311B.

C. Temple of Isis, Philae. Open lotus. 300 BC – AD 200. See page 194, 311A, 312A.

D. Temple of Isis, Philae. Open lotus. 300 BC – AD 200. See page 311C.

A. Temple of Isis, Philae. Open lotus. 300 BC – AD 200.

B. Temple of Isis, Philae. Open lotus. 300 BC – AD 200. See page 312D, 313B.

C. Temple of Haroeris and Sobek, Kom Ombo. Open lotus. 180–145 BC. See page 142, 313D.

D. Temple of Haroeris and Sobek, Kom Ombo. Open lotus. 180–145 BC. See page 142, 310B, 313D.

A. Precinct of Amun, Karnak, Luxor. Closed papyrus. 1290–1213 BC. See page 187.

B. Temple of Haroeris and Sobek, Kom Ombo. Open lotus. 180–145 BC. See page 142.

C. Precinct of Amun, Karnak, Luxor. Closed papyrus. 1290–1213 BC. See page 186.

D. Temple of Isis, Philae. Open papyrus. 300 BC – AD 200. See page 311D, 312C, 313A.

A. Temple of Isis, Philae. Open papyrus. 300 BC – AD 200. See page 310C.

B. Temple of Haroeris and Sobek, Kom Ombo. Open papyrus, 180–145 BC.

C. Temple of Isis, Philae. Open papyrus. 300 BC – AD 200.

D. Temple of Horus, Edfu. Open papyrus. 145 BC. See page 159.

A. Temple of Horus, Edfu. Open papyrus. 145 BC. See page 159.

B. Temple of Isis, Philae. Palm. 300 BC – AD 200.

C. Precinct of Amun, Karnak, Luxor. Open papyrus. 1290–1213 BC. See page 185.

D. Temple of Haroeris and Sobek, Kom Ombo. Palm. 180–145 BC.

A. Temple of Isis, Philae. Hathor. 300 BC – AD 200. See page 196.

B. Temple of Isis, Philae. Hathor. 300 BC – AD 200. See page 196.

C. Temple of Isis, Philae. Hathor. 300 BC – AD 200. See page 196, 310C.

D. Temple of Isis, Philae. Hathor. 300 BC – AD 200. See page 192.

A. Luxor Temple, Luxor. Tentpole. 1279–1213 BC. See page 288A.

B. Hatshepsut Temple, Deir al-Bahari. Hathor column. 1473–1458 BC.

C. Hatshepsut Temple, Deir al-Bahari. 2050 BC.

D. Sultan al-Nasir Muhammad Mosque, the Citadel, Cairo. Reused red granite pharaonic column. See page 18.

A. Sultan al-Nasir Muhammad Mosque, the Citadel, Cairo. Reused pharaonic column.

B. Sultan al-Nasir Muhammad Mosque, the Citadel, Cairo. Reused Roman column. See page 16.

C. Sultan al-Nasir Muhammad Mosque, the Citadel, Cairo. Reused pharaonic column. See page 18.

D. Sultan al-Nasir Muhammad Mosque, the Citadel, Cairo.

A. The Hanging Church (al-Muʻallaqa), Old Cairo. See page 28.

B. Muhammad ʻAli Mosque, the Citadel, Cairo. Ottoman, 1830–1848. See page 10.

C. The Hanging Church (al-Muʻallaqa), Old Cairo. See page 28, 239B.

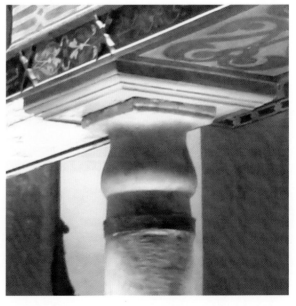

D. The Hanging Church (al-Muʻallaqa), Old Cairo. See page 24.

A. Sultan al-Nasir Muhammad Mosque, the Citadel, Cairo. Reused Roman composite (Corinthian) column. See page 16.

B. Sultan al-Nasir Muhammad Mosque, the Citadel, Cairo. Reused Coptic column.

C. Sultan al-Nasir Muhammad Mosque, the Citadel, Cairo. Reused Roman composite (Corinthian) column. See page 16.

D. Sultan al-Nasir Muhammad Mosque, the Citadel, Cairo. Reused Roman composite (Corinthian) column. See page 16.

3
DETAILS AND SURFACES

A. Cairo. See page 272D.

B. Aswan. See page 273C.

C. Cairo. See page 272B.

D. Cairo. See page 271B, D.

A. Cairo. See page 271D.

B. Cairo. See page 271C.

C. Cairo. See page 273A.

D. Cairo. See page 272A.

A. Cairo. See page 273B.

B. Cairo. See page 271A.

C. Cairo. See page 273D.

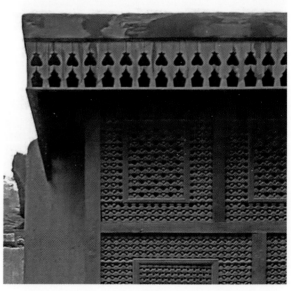

D. Cairo. See page 272C.

A. Cairo. See page 89.

B. Cairo. See page 89.

C. Cairo. See page 89.

D. Cairo. See page 89.

A. Temple of Isis, Philae. Palmettes, buds. 300 BC – AD 200. See page 294A.

B. Temple of Haroeris and Sobek, Kom Ombo. Papyrus, volutes. 300 BC – AD 200. See page 295D.

C. Temple of Isis, Philae. Lotus, papyrus. 300 BC – AD 200. See page 299C.

D. Temple of Haroeris and Sobek, Kom Ombo. Open papyrus. 300 BC – AD 200. See page 313D.

A. Temple of Isis, Philae. Papyrus, volutes. 300 BC – AD 200. See page 294C.

B. Temple of Isis, Philae. Palmettes, buds, papyrus. 300 BC – AD 200. See page 294B.

C. Temple of Isis, Philae. Palmettes, papyrus. 300 BC – AD 200. See page 294D.

D. Temple of Isis, Philae. Palmettes, buds, papyrus. 300 BC – AD 200. See page 296D.

A. Temple of Isis, Philae. Papyrus, volutes. 300 BC – AD 200. See page 194, 294C.

B. Temple of Isis, Philae. Papyrus. 300 BC – AD 200.

C. Temple of Isis, Philae. Papyrus. 300 BC – AD 200. See page 296D.

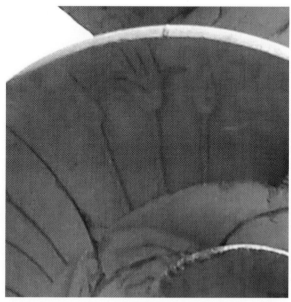

D. Temple of Isis, Philae. Lotus open, closed. 300 BC – AD 200. See page 295B.

A. Temple of Isis, Philae. Palmettes, buds. 300 BC – AD 200. See page 194, 296D.

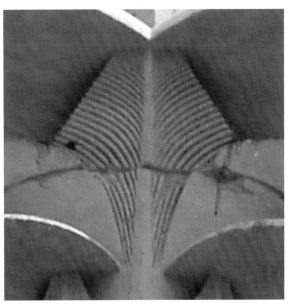

B. Temple of Isis, Philae. Palmettes. 300 BC – AD 200. See page 295B.

C. Temple of Isis, Philae. Palmettes, buds. 300 BC – AD 200. See page 294A.

D. Temple of Haroeris and Sobek, Kom Ombo. Open papyrus. 180–145 BC. See page 295C, 310D.

A. Queen Hatshepsut, Deir al-Bahari Temple. Circa 1450 BC.

B. Colossus of Ramesses II, Memphis. Limestone. 1290–1224 BC. See page 317.

C. Colossus of Ramesses II, Temple of Ramesses II, Abu Simbel. Sandstone.1244 BC. See page 132, 319.

D. Colossus of Ramesses II, Luxor Temple, Luxor. Granodiorite. 1244 BC. See page 172, 318.

A. Colossus of Ramesses II, Hathor Temple of Queen Nefertari, Abu Simbel. 1244 BC. See page 133.

B. Pillar fronted by statue of Ramesses II, Ramesses Temple, Abu Simbel. 1244 BC. See page 138.

C. Hathor, Hatshepsut Temple, Deir al-Bahari. Circa 1450 BC.

D. Ramesses II or Tutankhamun, Precinct of Amun, Karnak, Luxor.

A. Horus, Ramesses Temple, Abu Simbel. 1244 BC. See page 132.

B. Ramesses Temple, Abu Simbel. 1244 BC. See page 132, 134.

C. Ram, Precinct of Amun, Karnak, Luxor. 650 BC. See page 182.

D. Queen Nefertari, Ramesses Temple, Abu Simbel. 1244 BC. See page 132, 134.

A. Colossus of Ramesses II, Memphis. Limestone. See page 314B.

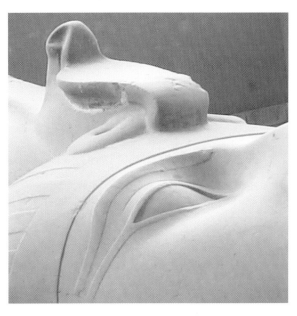

B. Colossus of Ramesses II, Memphis. Limestone. See page 314B.

C. Colossus of Ramesses II, Memphis. Limestone. See page 314B.

D. Colossus of Ramesses II, Memphis. Limestone. See page 314B.

A. Colossus of Ramesses II, Luxor. Granodiorite. See page 314D.

B. Colossus of Ramesses II, Luxor. Granodiorite. See page 314D.

C. Colossus of Ramesses II, Luxor. Granodiorite. See page 314D.

D. Colossus of Ramesses II, Luxor. Granodiorite. See page 314D.

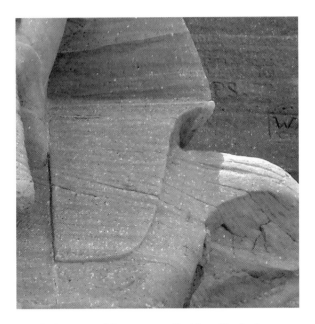

A. Colossus of Ramesses II, Abu Simbel. Sandstone. See page 314C.

B. Colossus of Ramesses II, Abu Simbel. Sandstone. See page 314C.

C. Colossus of Ramesses II, Abu Simbel. Sandstone. See page 314C.

D. Colossus of Ramesses II, Abu Simbel. Sandstone. See page 314C.

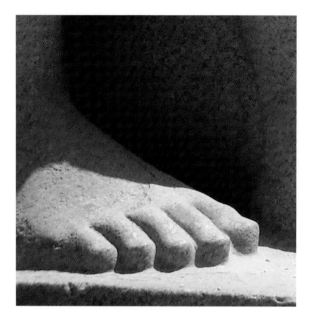

A. Colossus of Ramesses II, Luxor. Granodiorite. See page 174.

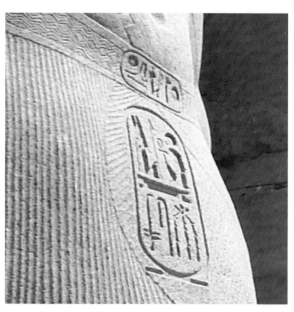

B. Colossus of Ramesses II, Luxor. Granodiorite. See page 174.

C. Colossus of Ramesses II, Luxor. Granodiorite. See page 174.

D. Colossus of Ramesses II, Luxor. Granodiorite. See page 174.

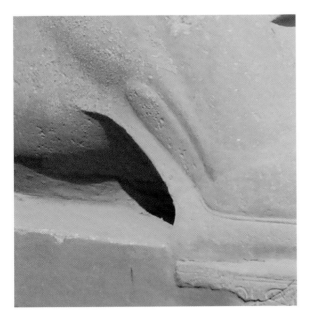

A. Ram, Precinct of Amun, Karnak, Luxor. See page 182.

B. Temple of Haroeris and Sobek, Kom Ombo. See page 150.

C. Temple of Ramesses II, Abu Simbel. See page 136.

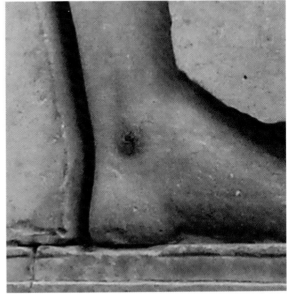

D. Temple of Haroeris and Sobek, Kom Ombo. See page 150.

A. Temple of Haroeris and Sobek, Kom Ombo. See page 150.

B. Temple of Haroeris and Sobek, Kom Ombo. See page 150.

C. Temple of Haroeris and Sobek, Kom Ombo. See page 150.

D. Temple of Haroeris and Sobek, Kom Ombo. See page 150.

A. Sekhmet, Temple of Haroeris and Sobek, Kom Ombo. See page 148.

B. Sekhmet, Temple of Haroeris and Sobek, Kom Ombo. See page 148.

C. Sekhmet, Temple of Haroeris and Sobek, Kom Ombo. See page 148.

D. Sekhmet, Temple of Haroeris and Sobek, Kom Ombo. See page 148.

A. Temple of Isis, Philae. See page 198.

B. Image A enlarged.

C. Image A enlarged.

D. Image A enlarged.

A. Temple of Isis, Philae. See page 198.

B. Temple of Isis, Philae. See page 198.

C. Sekhmet, Temple of Haroeris and Sobek, Kom Ombo.

D. Temple of Isis, Philae. See page 198.

A. Temple of Horus, Edfu. See page 164.

B. Temple of Horus, Edfu. See page 164.

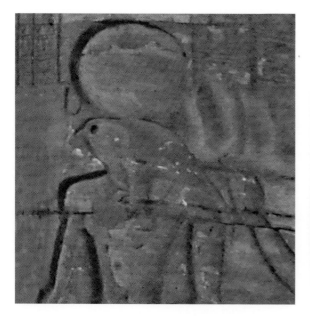

C. Temple of Haroeris and Sobek, Kom Ombo.

D. Luxor Temple.

A. Luxor Temple. See page 174.

B. Luxor Temple. See page 174.

C. Luxor Temple. See page 174.

D. Luxor Temple.

A. Ramesses Temple, Abu Simbel. See page 134.

B. Ramesses Temple, Abu Simbel. See page 136, 329D.

C. Ramesses Temple, Abu Simbel. See page 136.

D. Image C enlarged.

A. Temple of Haroeris and Sobek, Kom Ombo.

B. Temple of Haroeris and Sobek, Kom Ombo. See page 144.

C. Temple of Isis, Philae. See page 192.

D. Sun Temple, Abu Simbel. See page 136, 328B.

A. Cartouche, Temple of Horus, Edfu. See page 162.

B. Cartouches, Sun Temple, Abu Simbel. See page 136.

C. Cartouche, Temple of Haroeris and Sobek, Kom Ombo.

D. Cartouches, Temple of Isis, Philae. See page 196.

A. Ankh. Temple of Haroeris and Sobek, Kom Ombo. See page 145. Temple of Horus, Edfu. See page 160.

B. Temple of Isis, Philae. See page 196.

C. Temple of Horus, Edfu. See page 159.

D. Ramesses Temple, Abu Simbel. See page 136.

A. Closed lotus frieze, Temple of Horus, Edfu. See page 162.

B. Temple of Horus, Edfu. See page 162.

C. Temple of Horus, Edfu. See page 162.

D. Temple of Horus, Edfu. See page 162.

A. Temple of Horus, Edfu. See page 162.

B. Temple of Horus, Edfu. See page 162.

C. Temple of Horus, Edfu. See page 162.

D. Temple of Horus, Edfu. See page 162.

A. Temple of Haroeris and Sobek, Kom Ombo. See page 148.

B. Temple of Haroeris and Sobek, Kom Ombo. See page 148.

C. Temple of Haroeris and Sobek, Kom Ombo. See page 148.

D. Temple of Haroeris and Sobek, Kom Ombo. See page 148.

A. Temple of Haroeris and Sobek, Kom Ombo.

B. Temple of Haroeris and Sobek, Kom Ombo.

C. Temple of Haroeris and Sobek, Kom Ombo.

D. Temple of Haroeris and Sobek, Kom Ombo.

A. Temple of Haroeris and Sobek, Kom Ombo. See page 146.

B. Temple of Haroeris and Sobek, Kom Ombo. See page 146.

C. Temple of Haroeris and Sobek, Kom Ombo. See page 146.

D. Temple of Haroeris and Sobek, Kom Ombo. See page 146.

A. Temple of Haroeris and Sobek, Kom Ombo. See page 146.

B. Temple of Haroeris and Sobek, Kom Ombo. See page 146.

C. Temple of Haroeris and Sobek, Kom Ombo. See page 146.

D. Temple of Haroeris and Sobek, Kom Ombo. See page 146.

A. Baboon frieze, Ramesses Temple, Abu Simbel. See page 132.

B. Cobra frieze, Temple of Haroeris and Sobek, Kom Ombo. See page 142.

C. Sun disk flanked by uraeus, Temple of Haroeris and Sobek, Kom Ombo. See page 142.

D. Hathor frieze, Temple of Isis, Philae. See page 200, 245B.

A. Sofitel Hotel, Sharm al-Sheikh. Modern muqarnas in wood.

B. al-Azhar Mosque, Cairo. Muqarnas in stone. See page 259C, D.

C. al-Azhar Mosque, Cairo. Muqarnas in stone. See page 259A.

D. Ben Ezra Synagogue, Old Cairo. Muqarnas in stone. See page 279D.

E. Sayyidna al-Hussein Mosque, Cairo.

F. Temple of Isis, Philae. See page 200, 245B.

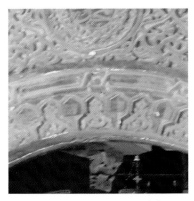

G. Hanging Church, Old Cairo. See page 239C.

H. Hanging Church, Old Cairo. See page 239B.

I. Hanging Church, Old Cairo. See page 239C.

A. al-Azhar Mosque, Cairo. See page 259A, 246C.

B. al-Azhar Mosque, Cairo. See page 240B.

C. Sabil-Kuttab of Tusun Pasha, Cairo. See page 100, 240A, 260A.

D. Gate of the Wikala of al-Ghuri in the Khan al-Khalili Bazaar, Cairo. See page 232A.

E. Greek Orthodox Church of St. George, Old Cairo. See page 248B.

F. Doorway in Old Cairo. See page 38, 241B.

G. al-Azhar Mosque, Cairo. See page 248B.

H. The Egyptian Museum, Cairo. See page 240C.

I. Sayyidna al-Hussein Mosque, Cairo. See page 239A.

A. The Sabil of Nafisa al-Bayda, Cairo. See page 102.

B. Sayyidna al-Hussein Mosque, Cairo. See page 239A.

C. The Sabil of Nafisa al-Bayda, Cairo. See page 261A.

D. Badistan Gate, Khan al-Khalili Bazaar. See page 46, 233B.

E. Gate of al-Ghuri, Khan al-Khalili Bazaar. See page 48 and 232B.

F. Badistan Gate, Khan al-Khalili Bazaar. See page 46, 232C.

G. al-Mu'izz li-Din Allah Street, Cairo.

H. Old Cataract Hotel, Aswan. See page 234C.

I. Doorway in Old Cairo. See page 38, 241D.

A. Doorway in Old Cairo. See page 36, 241D.

B. Doorway in Old Cairo. See page 36, 241D.

C. Doorway in Old Cairo. See page 36, 241D.

D. Doorway in Old Cairo. See page 36, 241D.

E. The Hanging Church, Old Cairo. See page 29, 239B.

F. The Sabil of Nafisa al-Bayda, Cairo. See page 102.

G. Doorway in Old Cairo. See page 38, 241B.

H. The Sabil of Nafisa al-Bayda, Cairo. See page 102.

I. Temple of Isis, Philae. See page 200, 245B.

A. Residential al-Mu'izz li-Din Allah Street, Cairo.

B. al-Azhar Mosque, Cairo. See page 246C, 259A.

C. al-Mu'izz li-Din Allah Street, Cairo.

D. St. Catherine's Monastery, Mount Sinai. See page 221.

E. St. Catherine's Monastery, Mount Sinai. See page 221.

F. St. Catherine's Monastery, Mount Sinai. See page 221.

G. Temple of Isis, Philae. See page 200, 245B.

H. St. Catherine's Monastery, Mount Sinai. See page 221.

I. Church of Saints Sergius and Bacchus, Old Cairo. See page 42.

A. The Sabil of Nafisa al-Bayda, Cairo. See page 102.

B. The Hanging Church, Old Cairo. See page 28, 239B, C.

C. The Sabil of Nafisa al-Bayda, Cairo. See page 102, 261A.

D. al-Azhar Mosque, Cairo. See page 240B.

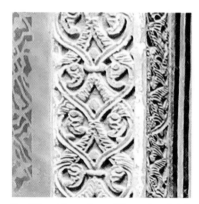

E. The Hanging Church, Old Cairo. See page 28.

F. Doorway in Old Cairo. See page 38, 241B.

G. Sayyidna al-Hussein Mosque, Cairo. See page 239A.

H. al-Azhar Mosque, Cairo. See page 240B.

I. Doorway in Old Cairo. See page 38, 241B.

A. The Hanging Church, Old Cairo. See page 28, 239B.

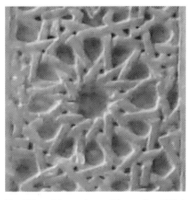

B. The Hanging Church, Old Cairo. See page 28, 239B, C.

C. The Hanging Church, Old Cairo. See page 28, 239B, C.

D. al-Azhar Mosque, Cairo. See page 246A, 259B.

E. The Hanging Church, Old Cairo. See page 28, 239B.

F. al-Azhar Mosque, Cairo. See page 246A, 259B.

G. The Hanging Church, Old Cairo. See page 239C.

H. The Hanging Church, Old Cairo. See page 28, 239B.

I. The Hanging Church, Old Cairo. See page 239C.

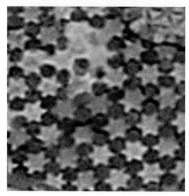

A. Abu al-Haggag Mosque, Luxor. See page 108, 258D.

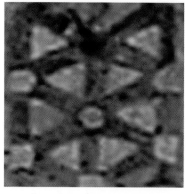

B. Abu al-Haggag Mosque, Luxor. See page 108, 258D.

C. Abu al-Haggag Mosque, Luxor. See page 108, 258D.

D. The Hanging Church, Old Cairo. See page 28, 239B.

E. Sultan al-Nasir Muhammad Mosque, Cairo. See page 238A.

F. The Hanging Church, Old Cairo. See page 28.

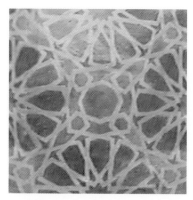

G. The Hanging Church, Old Cairo. See page 28.

H. The Hanging Church, Old Cairo. See page 28.

I. The Hanging Church, Old Cairo. See page 28, 239B.

A. See page 272C.

B. See page 80.

C. See page 68.

D. See page 68.

E. See page 272C.

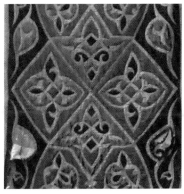

F. See page 61.

G. See page 68.

H. See page 46.

I. See page 102.

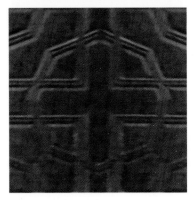

A. Cross panel.

B. Knot.

C. Door, the Hanging Church, Old Cairo. See page 239B.

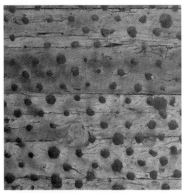

D. Doorway, Old Cairo. See page 241C.

E. Sofitel Hotel, Sharm al-Sheikh.

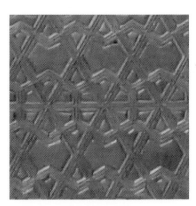

F. Door, the Hanging Church, Old Cairo. See page 239B.

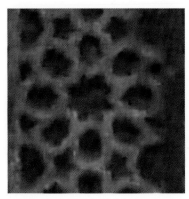

G. Typical Islamic geometric pattern.

H. Stylized floral, Sofitel Hotel, Sharm al-Sheikh.

I. Door, the Hanging Church, Old Cairo. See page 22.

A. Image E enlarged.

B. The Hanging Church, Old Cairo.

C. Image E enlarged.

D. Greek Orthodox Church of St. George, Old Cairo. See page 34, 241A.

E. Ivory and wood cross motif, the Hanging Church, Old Cairo. See page 24, 26.

F. Greek Orthodox Church of St. George, Old Cairo. See page 34, 241A.

G. The Hanging Church, Old Cairo. See page 26, 239C.

H. Image E enlarged.

I. Image E enlarged.

A. Sayyidna al-Hussein Mosque, Cairo. See page 239D.

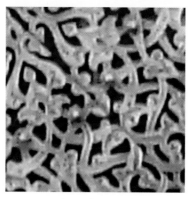

B. Sayyidna al-Hussein Mosque, Cairo. See page 239D.

C. Sayyidna al-Hussein Mosque, Cairo. See page 239D.

D. Sayyidna al-Hussein Mosque, Cairo. See page 239D.

E. Sayyidna al-Hussein Mosque, Cairo. See page 239D.

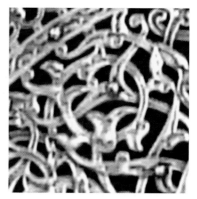

F. Sayyidna al-Hussein Mosque, Cairo. See page 239D.

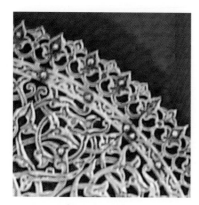

G. Sayyidna al-Hussein Mosque, Cairo. See page 239D.

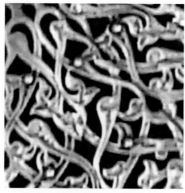

H. Sayyidna al-Hussein Mosque, Cairo. See page 239D.

I. Sayyidna al-Hussein Mosque, Cairo. See page 239D.

A. Sayyidna al-Hussein Mosque, Cairo. See page 239A.

B. Sayyidna al-Hussein Mosque, Cairo. See page 239A.

C. Sayyidna al-Hussein Mosque, Cairo. See page 239A.

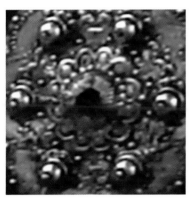

D. Sayyidna al-Hussein Mosque, Cairo. See page 239A.

E. Sayyidna al-Hussein Mosque, Cairo. See page 239A.

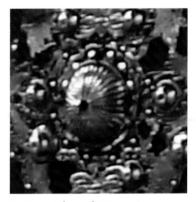

F. Sayyidna al-Hussein Mosque, Cairo. See page 239A.

G. Sayyidna al-Hussein Mosque, Cairo. See page 239A.

H. Sayyidna al-Hussein Mosque, Cairo. See page 239A.

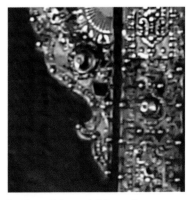

I. Sayyidna al-Hussein Mosque, Cairo. See page 239A.

A. See page 247A, D, 253A.

B. See page 247C.

C. See page 247A, D, 253A.

D. Image B, C, G enlarged. See page 247D, 253A.

E. Image G enlarged. See page 247C.

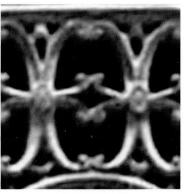

F. Image B, G enlarged. See page 247C, 253A.

G. See page 247C.

H. See page 246D, 256D, 260A.

I. Image C enlarged. See 247A, D, 253A.

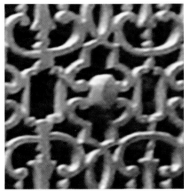

A. Image E enlarged. See page 247B.

B. See page 254D.

C. See page 253C.

D. See page 42, 253B.

E. See page 102, 247B.

F. Image E enlarged. See page 247B.

G. Turned wood mashrabiyya in window.

H. See page 254D.

I. See page 250C, 255C.

A. Sinai. See page 226.

B. Cairo. See page 94.

C. Abu Simbel. See page 132.

D. Sinai. See page 228.

E. Sinai. See page 228.

F. Cairo. See page 94.

G. Sinai. See page 228.

H. Sinai. See page 228.

I. Sinai. See page 226.

A. Old Cairo. See page 36, 241D.

B. Giza.

C. Old Cairo. See page 36, 241D.

D. Old Cairo. See page 36, 241D.

E. The Sphinx, sandstone, Giza. See page 118.

F. Old Cairo. See page 36.

G. Old Cairo. See page 40.

H. Sinai. See page 229.

I. Sinai. See page 208.

A. Khan al-Khalili, Cairo. See page 48.

B. Giza. See page 118.

C. Abu al-Haggag Mosque, Luxor. See page 106.

D. Abu al-Haggag Mosque, Luxor.

E. Khan al-Khalili, Cairo. See page 46.

F. Cairo. See page 74.

G. Abu Simbel.

H. Cairo.

I. Abu al-Haggag Mosque, Luxor.

A. Saqqara

B. Saqqara. See page 126.

C. Sinai. See page 208.

D. Sinai.

E. Saqqara. See page 126.

F. Sinai.

G. Giza.

H. Sinai. See page 208.

I. St. Catherine's Monastery. See page 242C.

357

A. Hotel, Bahariya Oasis, Western Desert.

B. Sinai.

C. Cairo

D. St. Catherine's Monastery. See page 220.

E. St. Catherine's Monastery. See page 218.

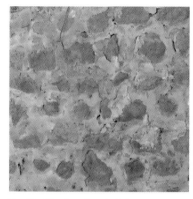

F. St. Catherine's Monastery. See page 225.

G. Sinai.

H. St. Catherine's Monastery. See page 224.

I. Old Cairo. See page 30.

A. Sinai.

B. St. Catherine's Monastery.

C. St. Catherine's Monastery.

D. St. Catherine's Monastery. See page 228.

E. St. Catherine's Monastery. See page 218.

F. St. Catherine's Monastery. See page 228.

G. St. Catherine's Monastery.

H. St. Catherine's Monastery.

I. Saqqara. See page 126.

359

A. Saqqara. See page 126.

B. Giza. See page 114.

C. Cairo. See page 42.

D. Giza. See page 118.

E. Giza. See page 118.

F. St. Catherine's Monastery. See page 221.

G. St. Catherine's Monastery. See page 218.

H. Cairo.

I. Giza. See page 114.

A. Cairo. See page 89.

B. Karnak. See page 182.

C. Cairo. See page 89.

D. Cairo.

E. Cairo. See page 89.

F. Cairo. See page 96.

G. Cairo. See page 84.

H. Cairo. See page 86.

I. Cairo. See page 96.

A. St. Catherine's Monastery. See page 218.

B. Giza. See page 118.

C. St. Catherine's Monastery. See page 221.

D. St. Catherine's Monastery.

E. Saqqara. See page 126.

F. Old Cairo. See page 40.

G. Saqqara. See page 124.

H. Luxor.

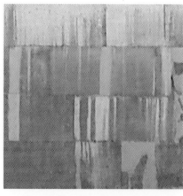

I. Saqqara. See page 124.

A. Cairo.

B. Cairo.

C. Cairo.

D. Cairo.

E. Old Cairo. See page 36, 241D.

F. Old Cairo. See page 40.

G. Cairo.

H. Cairo. See page 285B.

I. Cairo.

A. St. Catherine's Monastery. See page 221.

B. Cairo. See page 89.

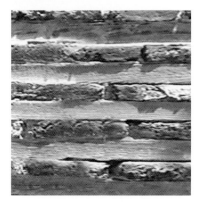

C. Old Cairo. See page 42.

D. Cairo.

E. Cairo.

F. Cairo. See page 51.

G. Cairo.

H. Cairo. See page 250C.

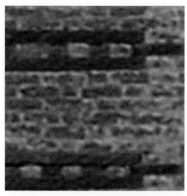

I. Luxor Temple. See page 258D.

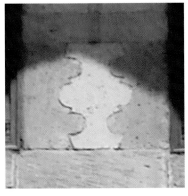

A. Khan al-Khalili. See page 46.

B. Cairo. See page 94.

C. Cairo. See page 253C.

D. Old Cairo. See page 36, 241A.

E. Cairo. See page 239D.

F. Cairo. See page 240C, D.

G. Cairo. See page 96, 249A.

H. Cairo.

I. Cairo. See page 78.

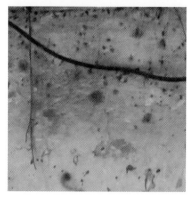

A. Cairo. See page 80.

B. Cairo. See page 94.

C. Cairo. See page 226.

D. Cairo. See page 74.

E. Cairo. See page 40.

F. Cairo. See page 74.

G. Cairo. See page 74.

H. Cairo. See page 226.

I. Cairo. See page 74.

A. Cairo. See page 90.

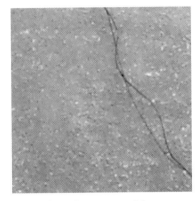

B. Cairo. See page 89.

C. Cairo. See page 40.

D. Bahariya Oasis, Western Desert.

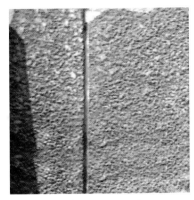

E. Cairo. See page 72.

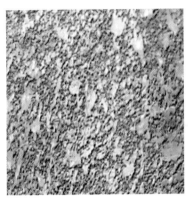

F. Cairo. See page 96.

G. Luxor. See page 78.

H. Cairo. See page 96.

I. Cairo. See page 78.

A. Khan al-Khalili, Cairo. See page 50.

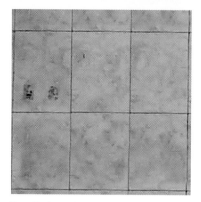

B. Cairo. See page 72.

C. Cairo.

D. St. Catherine's Monastery. See page 224.

E. Giza. See page 118.

F. Giza.

G. Cairo.

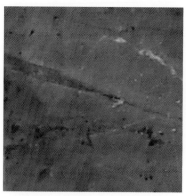

H. Cairo. See page 265C.

I. Giza. See page 243D.

A. Sinai.

B. Sinai.

C. Sinai.

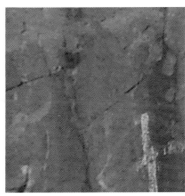

D. Sinai. See page 208.

E. Giza.

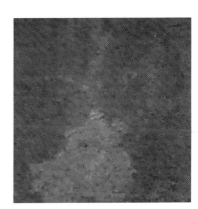

F. Sinai.

G. Sinai. See page 210.

H. Sinai.

I. Sinai.

A. Sinai.

B. Sinai.

C. Giza.

D. Giza.

E. Sinai.

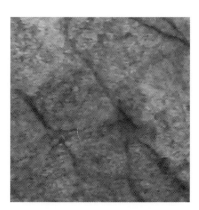

F. Sinai.

G. Sinai.

H. Sinai.

I. Sinai.

A. Sinai. See page 210.

B. Sinai.

C. Sinai. See page 210.

D. Sinai. See page 206.

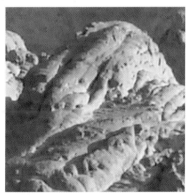

E. Sinai. See page 212.

F. Sinai. See page 206.

G. Sinai.

H. Sinai. See page 216.

I. Sinai. See page 213.

4

GRAPHICS

A. Luxor. See page 80.

B. Luxor. See page 86.

C. Khan al-Khalili, Cairo. See page 56.

A. Luxor. See page 86.

B. Khan al-Khalili, Cairo. See page 56.

C. Luxor. See page 84.

A. Bahariya Oasis, Western Desert. See page 76.

B. Luxor. See page 82.

C. Cairo. See page 62. (Arabic script is reversed on transparent banner.)

D. Luxor. See page 86.

E. Khan al-Khalili, Cairo. See page 56.

F. Khan al-Khalili, Cairo. See page 56.

A. Luxor. See page 82.

B. Luxor. See page 86.

C. Luxor. See page 86.

D. Luxor. See page 88.

A. Khan al-Khalili, Cairo. See page 56.

B. Luxor. See page 88.

C. Luxor. See page 256D.

D. Luxor. See page 84.

A. Cairo. See page 100.

B. Cairo.

C. Cairo. See page 102.

D. Street sign, Cairo.

E. Old Cairo. See page 29.

F. Cairo. See page 94.

G. Street Sign, Cairo.

H. Old Cairo. See page 40.

I. Bahariya Oasis, Western Desert. See page 76.

A. Cairo. See page 72.

B. Cairo. See page 70.

C. Cairo. See page 70.

D. Cairo. See page 72.

E. Cairo. See page 102.

F. Cairo. See page 72.

G. Cairo. See page 54.

H. Cairo. See page 72.

I. Luxor. See page 88.

A. Cairo. See page 74.

B. Cairo. See page 98.

C. Luxor. See page 84.

D. Luxor. See page 84.

E. Luxor. See page 78.

F. Luxor. See page 86.

G. Khan al-Khalili, Cairo.
See page 50.

H. Khan al-Khalili, Cairo.
See page 50.

I. Luxor. See page 82.

A. Luxor. See page 84.

B. Luxor.

C. Luxor. See page 84.

D. Bahariya Oasis, Western Desert. See page 76.

A. Khan al-Khalili, Cairo. See page 50.

B. Khan al-Khalili, Cairo. See page 50.

C. Bahariya Oasis, Western Desert. See page 76.

D. Bahariya Oasis, Western Desert. See page 76.

BIBLIOGRAPHY

Baines, John and Jaromír Málek, *Atlas of Ancient Egypt*. Cairo: The American University in Cairo Press, 2002.

Behrens-Abouseif, Doris. *Cairo of the Mamluks: A History of the Architecture and Its Culture*. Cairo: The American University in Cairo Press, 2007.

Behrens-Abouseif, Doris. *The Minarets of Cairo: Islamic Architecture from the Arab Conquest to the End of the Ottoman Empire*. Cairo: The American University in Cairo Press, 2010.

Ludwig, Carolyn, editor. *The Churches of Egypt: From the Journey of the Holy Family to the Present Day*. Cairo: The American University in Cairo Press, 2007.

O'Kane, Bernard, editor. *Creswell Photographs Re-examined: New Perspectives on Islamic Architecture*. Cairo: The American University in Cairo Press, 2009.

Prisse D'Avennes, E. *Atlas of Egyptian Art*. Cairo: The American University in Cairo Press, 2000.

Warner, Nicholas. *The Monuments of Historic Cairo: A Map and Descriptive Guide*. Cairo: The American University in Cairo Press, 2005.

Williams, Caroline. *Islamic Monuments in Cairo: The Practical Guide*. Sixth edition, Cairo: The American University in Cairo Press, 2008.

CHRONOLOGY

Early Dynastic Period (2950–2575 BC)

Dynasties 1–3

    Djoser

Old Kingdom (2575–2150 BC)

Dynasties 4–8

    Snefru

    Khufu

    Khafre

    Menkaure

First Intermediate Period (2125–1975 BC)

Dynasties 9–11

Middle Kingdom (1975–1640 BC)

Dynasties 12–14

Second Intermediate Period (1630–1075 BC)

Dynasties 15–17

New Kingdom (1539–1292 BC)

Dynasties 18–20

    Hatshepsut

    Amenhotep IV/Akhenaten

    Tutankhamun

    Sety I

    Ramesses II

    Ramesses III

Third Intermediate Period (1075–715 BC)

Dynasties 21–25

Late Period (715–332 BC)

Dynasties 25–30

Greco-Roman Period (332 BC–AD 395)

    Ptolemy VI

    Ptolemy VII

    Ptolemy IX

    Cleopatra

Byzantine Period (AD 395–639)

Islamic Conquest of Egypt by Amr ibn al-As (640–641)

Umayyads (661–750)

Abbasids (750–868)

Tulunids (868–905)

Ikhshidids (935–969)

Fatimids (969–1171)

Ayyubids (1171–1250)

Mamluks (1250–1517)

    Qalawun

    al-Nasir Muhammad

    Sultan Hasan

    al-Mu'ayyad Shaykh

    Qaytbay

    al-Ghuri

Ottoman Period (1517–1798)

Napoleonic Invasion (1798–1801)

Muhammad 'Ali Dynasty (1805–1952)

    Muhammad 'Ali

    Farouk

Republic (1953 – present)